T0316774

The Effect of the War on the External Trade of the United Kingdom

THE EFFECT OF THE WAR ON THE EXTERNAL TRADE OF THE UNITED KINGDOM

AN ANALYSIS OF THE MONTHLY STATISTICS, 1906—1914

BY

A. L. BOWLEY, Sc.D.

Professor of Statistics in the University of London

Cambridge :

at the University Press

1915

CAMBRIDGE
UNIVERSITY PRESS

University Printing House, Cambridge CB2 8BS, United Kingdom

Cambridge University Press is part of the University of Cambridge.

It furthers the University's mission by disseminating knowledge in the pursuit of education, learning and research at the highest international levels of excellence.

www.cambridge.org
Information on this title: www.cambridge.org/9781107433205

© Cambridge University Press 1915

First published 1915
First paperback edition 2014

A catalogue record for this publication is available from the British Library

ISBN 978-1-107-43320-5 Paperback

Additional resources for this publication at www.cambridge.org/9781107433205

PREFATORY NOTE

This essay contains the substance of four lectures, delivered at the London School of Economics and Political Science in January and February, 1915.

TABLE OF CONTENTS

DIAGRAMS AT END

Value of Imports of Produce into the United Kingdom, month by month, 1906–1914.

Value of Exports of Produce of the United Kingdom, month by month, and Re-exports of Foreign and Colonial Merchandise, 1906–1914.

CHAPTER I

VALUES OF IMPORTS AND EXPORTS IN THE AGGREGATE

(1) INTRODUCTORY

THE effect on the external trade of the United Kingdom of the declaration of war with Germany was immediate, considerable and far-reaching. When the first shock was exhausted, trade tended to adapt itself to the new conditions, and a fresh, though unstable, equilibrium was soon established; from this position it is not improbable that a healthy development may result, if there are no more sudden disturbances on a large scale. It is of great interest to observe in what way the shock took effect, and in what respects adjustments were made; and, though it is as yet much too soon to forecast the lines of growth or the probable quantity and quality of trade during the continuance of a state of war, it is still of great importance to set out the data we have and to envisage the problem. We are now living at so rapid a pace, that current events pass immediately into history and cease to afford guidance even for the near future; the historian must become journalist, the journalist merely reporter; and the statistician must forget his customary caution and hesitation, and offer, with a confidence that is more apparent than real, crude results and undigested opinions, if his work is to be of immediate practical service. This must be my excuse for what is badly formulated, or may prove to be incorrectly stated, in the following analysis.

To bring the subject into a manageable compass, it has seemed best to keep to those facts which are directly deducible from official trade statistics, not to go into great detail, and not to seek out reasons for the changes of supply, consumption, or price of special commodities.

(2) Former Course of Trade

To understand and to place in their proper setting the changes in external trade caused by the war, it is necessary to have a general acquaintance with the movement of imports and exports in recent years.

TRADE OF THE UNITED KINGDOM (bullion and specie excluded).

Value in £000,000s of

	Imports	Exports	Re-exports
		Produce of United Kingdom	Foreign and Colonial produce
1901	522	280	68
1902	528	283	66
1903	543	291	70
1904	551	301	70
1905	565	330	78
1906	608	376	85
1907	646	426	92
1908	593	377	80
1909	625	378	91
1910	678	430	104
1911	680	454	103
1912	745	487	112
1913	769	525	110
1914	697	430	95

After a brief inflation, mainly due to high prices, at the end of the nineteenth century, the aggregate values of imports and of exports were set back slightly in 1901, and from that date rose with acceleration to a maximum in 1907. In 1908 there was a fall, but not enough to reach the totals of 1905, and then the growth set in again and was continued (except in the case of exports of foreign and colonial goods) till and including 1913.

It is at once essential to know how far this growth was due to increased prices and how far to increased quantities of goods. This has been determined by well-known methods (which are explained and used on pp. 39 seq. below). Taking as pivotal dates 1901, the first year of our table, 1907 the year of temporary maximum and 1913, the last normal year, it is found that exports of home produce increased from the year 1901 to the year 1907 43 per cent. in quantity and a further 7 per cent. in value owing to higher prices, and from 1907 to 1913 14 per cent. in quantity and a further 8 per cent. in value; every year except 1908 shows a considerable rise in quantity as well as in value, though prices did not move uniformly in the period. As regards imports (excluding goods subsequently exported) we also find an uninterrupted, though slower growth, except in 1908; from 1901 to 1907 the increase was 10 per cent. in quantity, with a further 11 per cent. from price, and from 1907 to 1913 16 per cent. with a further 3 per cent.

So far then as the aggregate annual statistics are concerned, there is no suggestion that 1913 had seen the climax of that growth of foreign trade, which has been so remarkable a feature of the industrial history of the last thirteen years; each year had continued to make new records in imports and in exports whether measured by value or by quantity. None the less anxiety was already felt by the end of 1913 as to the continuance of such satisfactory trade, and till we have determined whether these forebodings were being justified in the first half of 1914, we cannot measure the effect of the war. The monthly statistics of trade enable us to form a reasonable judgment on the matter. They are summarized in the following table; since they are given only to the nearest million or hundred thousand pounds, so as to present a general view of the whole mass, minor changes are concealed. The same figures are exhibited in the diagrams at the end of the book.

VALUES OF IMPORTS AND

(3) Classification and Presentation of the Monthly Statistics

Imports (*whether for consumption or re-export; bullion and specie excluded*).

Value in £000,000s.

Year	Jan.	Feb.	Mar.	April	May	June	July	Aug.	Sept.	Oct.	Nov.	Dec.	Year's total

Class I. *Food, drink and tobacco.*

Year	Jan.	Feb.	Mar.	April	May	June	July	Aug.	Sept.	Oct.	Nov.	Dec.	Year's total
1906	20	17	20	18	20	21	21	21	20	22	20	19	238
1907	20	16	20	20	20	21	22	22	20	24	22	21	248
1908	20	19	22	20	18	20	20	18	22	22	21	21	244
1909	19	17	21	22	18	23	22	22	23	21	24	23	254
1910	22	18	22	21	22	22	20	21	22	22	23	23	258
1911	21	18	20	19	21	21	22	23	23	25	27	25	264
1912	24	20	21	21	21	21	25	25	23	28	26	26	281
1913	22	21	22	24	23	24	26	24	25	27	26	26	290
1914	24	21	24	22	22	23	24	22	23	28	31	34	298
Average, 1906–13	21	18	21	20	20	22	22	22	22	24	24	23	260

Class II. *Raw materials.*

Year	Jan.	Feb.	Mar.	April	May	June	July	Aug.	Sept.	Oct.	Nov.	Dec.	Year's total
1906	20	18	19	16	17	14	15	14	13	19	22	23	211
1907	27	24	24	23	19	15	17	15	13	20	22	23	241
1908	25	21	17	15	14	15	14	13	13	16	17	23	203
1909	23	22	18	16	15	16	16	14	14	19	25	24	220
1910	22	20	22	25	20	20	17	17	17	22	28	32	261
1911	29	25	23	19	18	16	15	15	17	22	24	25	248
1912	27	25	24	24	19	15	18	18	18	25	29	32	276
1913	32	27	22	22	21	18	19	17	20	27	27	28	282
1914	28	25	25	22	20	19	19	14	14	14	15	21	236
Average, 1906–13	26	23	21	20	18	16	16	15	16	21	24	26	243

Class III. *Manufactured goods.*

Year	Jan.	Feb.	Mar.	April	May	June	July	Aug.	Sept.	Oct.	Nov.	Dec.	Year's total
1906	13	12	14	13	14	13	13	13	12	14	13	12	156
1907	14	12	14	14	13	12	14	13	12	13	13	12	155
1908	11	12	13	13	12	11	12	11	12	12	11	12	143
1909	11	11	13	11	12	13	13	12	13	12	13	13	148
1910	12	12	14	13	13	13	12	13	13	13	13	14	157
1911	13	13	15	13	15	13	14	13	14	14	14	14	165
1912	15	14	16	15	15	14	16	16	15	17	16	16	185
1913	17	16	17	17	16	15	17	15	16	17	15	16	194
1914	16	16	18	17	17	16	16	7	8	10	9	12	161
Average, 1906–13	13	13	14	13	14	13	14	13	13	14	14	14	163

Total, *including miscellaneous.*

Year	Jan.	Feb.	Mar.	April	May	June	July	Aug.	Sept.	Oct.	Nov.	Dec.	Year's total
1906	53	48	53	47	51	48	49	49	45	55	56	55	608
1907	61	53	58	57	53	48	52	49	45	58	57	56	646
1908	56	52	52	47	44	46	47	43	48	51	50	57	593
1909	53	50	52	49	45	52	50	48	49	53	62	61	625
1910	56	51	58	60	55	55	49	52	52	58	64	69	678
1911	63	56	59	52	54	51	51	51	54	61	65	65	680
1912	67	60	61	60	55	51	58	60	57	71	71	74	745
1913	71	64	61	63	61	58	62	56	61	72	68	71	769
1914	68	62	67	62	59	58	59	42	45	52	56	68	697
Average, 1906–13	60	54	57	54	52	51	52	51	51	60	62	63	668

EXPORTS (*produce of the United Kingdom*).

Value in £000,000s.

CLASS I. *Food, drink and tobacco.*

Year	Jan.	Feb.	Mar.	April	May	June	July	Aug.	Sept.	Oct.	Nov.	Dec.	Year's total
1906	1·5[1]	1·3	1·5	1·3	1·6	1·5	1·9	2·0	2·1	2·4	2·3	1·7	21·1
1907	1·5	1·4	1·4	1·5	1·6	1·7	2·3	2·3	2·3	2·4	2·4	1·9	22·7
1908	1·5	1·5	1·4	1·5	1·6	1·6	2·0	2·1	2·0	2·3	2·3	2·0	21·9
1909	1·5	1·5	1·7	1·6	1·7	1·8	2·2	2·1	2·3	2·4	2·5	2·0	23·3
1910	1·6	1·7	1·7	1·9	1·8	2·1	2·5	2·5	2·5	2·7	2·8	2·2	26·1
1911	2·0	1·9	2·2	1·8	2·1	2·1	2·2	2·2	3·0	3·6	3·3	2·6	29·0
1912	2·3	2·1	2·7	2·5	2·4	2·3	2·7	3·0	3·0	3·6	3·5	2·5	32·7
1913	2·3	2·1	2·1	2·3	2·3	2·4	2·8	2·8	3·2	3·3	3·9	3·1	32·6
1914	2·4	2·3	2·4	2·3	2·3	2·6	2·7	1·5	2·1	2·2	2·0	1·9	26·9
Average, 1906–13	1·8	1·7	1·8	1·8	1·9	1·9	2·3	2·4	2·6	2·8	2·9	2·3	26·2

CLASS II. *Raw materials.*

Year	Jan.	Feb.	Mar.	April	May	June	July	Aug.	Sept.	Oct.	Nov.	Dec.	Year's total
1906	3·3	3·1	3·6	3·3	4·0	3·3	3·9	3·8	3·6	4·1	3·7	3·5	43·2
1907	3·9	3·9	4·1	4·3	4·6	4·5	5·1	4·9	4·9	5·3	5·0	4·5	55·0
1908	4·3	4·3	4·2	4·2	4·8	4·1	4·8	4·3	4·4	4·8	4·2	4·3	52·8
1909	3·7	3·6	4·2	3·9	4·6	4·2	4·5	4·1	4·5	4·7	4·6	4·6	51·2
1910	4·0	3·9	4·4	4·7	4·5	4·8	4·4	4·5	4·7	4·6	4·4	4·5	53·3
1911	4·4	4·1	4·6	4·1	4·9	4·2	3·9	4·2	4·7	4·9	4·8	4·9	53·7
1912	4·9	4·9	2·7	2·4	5·8	4·7	5·8	5·6	5·5	6·1	5·7	5·4	59·4
1913	5·8	5·2	5·3	6·1	5·8	5·8	6·4	5·4	5·8	6·4	5·9	6·1	69·9
1914	6·0	5·7	5·9	5·3	5·9	5·4	6·2	2·9	3·5	3·7	3·0	3·3	56·7
Average, 1906–13	4·3	4·1	4·1	4·1	4·9	4·5	4·9	4·7	4·8	5·1	4·8	4·7	54·8

CLASS III. *Manufactured goods.*

Year	Jan.	Feb.	Mar.	April	May	June	July	Aug.	Sept.	Oct.	Nov.	Dec.	Year's total
1906	26	24	26	22	26	25	27	27	24	26	26	26	306
1907	29	26	29	28	30	26	33	30	28	30	28	26	342
1908	28	25	27	25	24	23	26	23	25	25	22	22	297
1909	23	22	25	23	23	23	28	25	25	26	25	26	297
1910	29	26	28	28	27	27	31	31	29	30	29	30	343
1911	31	29	33	29	30	29	28	29	29	34	32	30	362
1912	32	30	34	27	30	27	33	34	34	38	33	32	385
1913	37	32	33	34	35	34	37	35	32	36	34	32	412
1914	39	32	35	32	33	31	35	19	21	22	19	20	338
Average, 1906–13	29	27	29	27	28	27	30	29	28	31	29	28	343

TOTAL, *including miscellaneous.*

Year	Jan.	Feb.	Mar.	April	May	June	July	Aug.	Sept.	Oct.	Nov.	Dec.	Year's total
1906	31	29	32	27	32	31	33	33	31	33	33	31	376
1907	35	32	35	34	37	33	40	37	35	38	36	33	426
1908	34	32	33	31	31	29	34	30	32	33	29	29	377
1909	29	28	32	29	30	30	35	32	33	34	33	34	378
1910	35	32	34	35	34	35	38	39	37	38	37	37	430
1911	38	36	41	36	38	36	35	36	37	44	41	39	454
1912	40	37	41	33	39	35	42	44	43	48	43	41	487
1913	45	40	42	43	44	43	47	44	42	47	45	43	525
1914	48	41	45	40	42	40	44	24	27	29	25	26	430
Average, 1906–13	36	33	36	33	35	34	38	37	36	39	37	36	432

[1] *i.e.*, £1,500,000.

RE-EXPORTS, *of foreign and colonial produce.*

£000,000s.

Year	Jan.	Feb.	Mar.	April	May	June	July	Aug.	Sept.	Oct.	Nov.	Dec.	Year's total
1906	7·5[1]	8·0	7·3	7·3	7·1	7·2	6·1	6·9	5·5	7·1	7·3	7·8	85·1
1907	8·8	9·4	8·1	9·7	8·4	7·1	7·4	7·4	5·9	6·9	6·1	6·7	91·9
1908	6·6	7·5	6·0	6·8	6·4	6·0	6·3	6·8	5·3	7·1	6·7	8·2	79·6
1909	6·7	8·5	7·5	8·6	7·2	7·9	7·4	7·0	6·5	7·6	6·8	9·6	91·3
1910	8·1	10·2	8·5	11·8	8·3	8·4	8·2	8·1	6·8	8·0	7·5	9·9	103·8
1911	8·6	10·0	9·2	9·5	8·8	8·7	8·2	6·7	7·8	8·7	7·8	8·7	102·8
1912	9·6	10·7	10·9	10·1	10·8	5·7	7·1	10·0	8·0	10·0	9·6	9·2	111·7
1913	10·7	10·8	9·6	10·1	9·4	8·5	8·3	8·1	6·9	9·6	8·0	9·7	109·7
1914	9·6	10·2	9·5	10·8	10·4	8·8	7·8	4·4	5·3	7·2	5·6	5·9	95·5
Average, 1906–13	8·3	9·4	8·4	9·2	8·3	7·4	7·4	7·6	6·6	8·1	7·5	8·7	97·0

The statistics of foreign trade are issued about the eighth day of each month, and contain tables of the information that has reached the Customs House in time for tabulation. A certain proportion of ships that have begun to unload before the end of each month are not accounted for in that month, but the data are carried forward to the next. Thus the statistics for August 1914 contain items relating to July trade, as is seen on pp. 48 *seq.* below. Further, the monthly figures are subject to corrections which appear in the Annual Reports (published in the summer of each year) and are entered in the re-capitulated figures month by month in the following year; thus the corrected figures for December 1914 will not be issued till January 8th, 1916. In the tables here given sometimes the corrected and sometimes the uncorrected figures are used; the corrections seem always to be small, and (except for a few groups of commodities) practically negligible.

In the tables both monthly and annual totals are given to the nearest unit, and consequently the sum for the months may differ by one or two units from the entry for the year.

Before dealing with the tables it is well to explain the terms and classification used. Under imports are included all goods landed in the United Kingdom (including the Isle of Man) that have come from foreign countries or other parts of the Empire or from non-British fisheries, and form part of ordinary trade transactions, except goods transhipped under bond from one ship to another whether at the same port or across the country. Bullion and specie are separately accounted for. Personal luggage, ships' stores and coal, the value of the wrappings and cases containing goods and some minor items are included neither in imports nor in exports, nor of

[1] *i.e.*, £7,500,000.

course goods smuggled in or out. The very important trade in diamonds from South Africa, and to and from the continent, is very imperfectly recorded.

Under exports are included all goods removed from the United Kingdom, with the exceptions just named. Transhipments under bond are excluded. Under exports of Foreign and Colonial Produce are included only those goods which have undergone no process of manufacture or alteration (other than grading or blending) in the United Kingdom; it is indifferent whether they have gone through the country not under bond on a through bill of lading, or whether they have been imported, owned and resold by a broker or agent in the United Kingdom. All other exports are counted as of home produce. The line thus drawn is somewhat arbitrary and not very significant; for on the one hand the cost of merchanting, handling and transport of foreign goods must be paid for (so that the common practice of subtracting these goods at their value at time of *export* from imports to obtain "net imports" or "imports for consumption" is inaccurate), and on the other hand only a very small proportion of goods (other than coal) are completely of British origin; thus tea, though it may be warehoused for some time, blended and packed, is counted as completely of foreign origin, while sugar, if it has been refined at home, is reckoned as wholly home produce.

Just now it is specially important to realize that goods taken out of the British Government's stores and depots are not counted as exports, whether for the use of the British or the Allied forces, nor are goods bought by the Government and shipped directly on Government vessels. Other goods bought by or on behalf of the Allies are included as exports. Such gifts to the Government as that of wheat from Canada are excluded. The value of enemy's cargoes, sold in the United Kingdom, is included, that of the ships themselves excluded (since old ships bought are in general excluded). The sugar bought and imported by the Royal Commission is included. These distinctions are rather arbitrary and will have to be considered in relation to the balance of trade, which will be extremely complicated during the war. At present, it need only be remarked that the value of enemy's cargoes does not form part of this balance, and it is to be hoped that the trade accounts will show them separately.

The value of imports is intended to be taken after they have arrived in port and before any process of unloading has taken place, and, of course, before duty is paid; the value of exports is reckoned as after they have been loaded into the ships. It is believed that these values are in general accurately declared, though there are many minor sources of error, from ignorance of the facts, carelessness or misapprehension on the part of exporters or importers. None of these errors is likely to affect any of the conclusions to which our present study will lead. If all transport by sea was organized and effected by persons who were paid outside the United Kingdom, and if no loans were made (capital exported or imported) or interest or profits paid into or from the country, then the value of imports would in the long run equal that of exports[1]. As it is, the whole services of British shipping and of brokers and agents at home in moving goods across the seas must be paid by an excess of imports over exports, and this excess is further increased by whatever amount interest and profits due to the United Kingdom and capital newly invested therein is greater than capital exported and interest and profits paid out. In this balance bullion and specie must be included, as well as produce.

For summary purposes both imports and exports are divided into three main classes with a small residuum. The first contains food, drink and tobacco, whether in their natural condition or manufactured. Though some commodities (*e.g.*, starch and alcohol) are available equally for use in food or drink or in manufacturing processes, and the destination of animals is not always known, little practical uncertainty is found in the classification. The second and third classes consist respectively of "raw materials and articles mainly unmanufactured" and of "articles wholly or mainly manu-

[1] Apart from certain relatively small sums. The complete statement is too detailed for insertion here.

factured." The amount of manufacture that entitles goods to enter the third class must obviously be arbitrary and the position of the line drawn between the classes must be determined by examination of details, not by definition. A very primitive state of manufacture in fact is sufficient to obtain inclusion in the third class; thus, pig-iron, combed wool, thrown silk, coal-tar, and tanned or dressed leather, are classed as manufactured; on the other hand all grades of petroleum are counted unmanufactured. Thus some unmanufactured materials are very nearly ready for use, while an enormous quantity of manufactured goods must undergo many more processes before actual consumption[1]. It follows that the results of this division can only be used for preliminary observation and for very crude generalization, while for more refined purposes the actual commodities must be studied separately. The miscellaneous class contains "living animals not for food and horses," goods sent by parcels post, and a small undefined residuum. The totals for the three classes, and the totals for imports, exports and re-exports, are shown in the tables (pp. 4–6) and the diagrams (at the end of the book). For the diagrams the nearest £100,000 was marked, while the tables give (in general) only the nearest million.

We can now return to the question whether the statistics of the first seven months of 1914 showed signs of retrogression from the very brisk trade of 1913.

When we consider the monthly averages for the years 1906–13 (see pp. 4–6), and add mentally about 10 per cent. to all records for February to make them comparable with those for other months, we find considerable seasonal movements in imported raw materials and in the small totals for exported food, etc., less notable movements in imported food, etc., and exported raw materials, and very little movement in manufactures. If we were considering separate commodities the seasonal influence would, of course, be more evident.

---

[1] For a further analysis of manufactured goods, into three sub-classes typified by (1) yarn, pig-iron, (2) cloth, steel bars, (3) clothes, machinery; see *Second Series of Memoranda...on British and Foreign Trade*, etc., Cd. 2337 of 1904, pp. 325 *seq*. See also Cd. 4954 of 1909, pp. 48–9.

In the resulting averaged totals for imports, exports and re-exports the monthly changes are great enough to require attention, though the results for March and April are depressed and that of May inflated by the coal strike of 1912, June depressed by the dock strike of 1912, and some August trade is transferred to September by the railway strike of 1911.

(4) The Position in July 1914

From the tables or diagrams, we see that the total value of imports established a record for each month from July 1912 to July 1913, and again in September and October 1913 and in March 1914; the totals for the intervening and following months up to and including July 1914, were in no case far below the greatest recorded in corresponding months. Similarly the export totals established a record in every month from July 1912 to March 1914, except September and October 1913 where the failure was very slight; but from April to July 1914, there was a definite set back, though the totals were still very high as compared with 1912 and earlier years.

To consider trade prospects it is best for various reasons to isolate imported raw materials and exported manufactures. Prices have a specially great influence on the former and some high values were reached in particular months in 1910 and 1911 as well as in 1912 and 1913. Some falling off is perceptible from November 1913 to February 1914, when compared with the same months in previous years, but there was a recovery in March, large totals from April to June, and the total in July 1914 was just a maximum. Exported manufactures showed signs of weakness in the early autumn of 1913, but established a record for any month in January 1914 and also a record for March. From April to July, however, the totals were from about 7 to 9 per cent. lower than corresponding months in 1913, but as much higher than the months in 1912.

Prices of imported raw materials were about 3 per cent. lower in the aggregate of the first seven months of 1914 than in the corresponding months of 1913, so that the quantities taken together were very nearly the same in the two years (see pp. 40 *seq.*). But the prices realized by exported manufactures averaged the same in the two years, so that the fall shown in the summer was of quantity as well as of value.

Summing up this discussion we may say that trade as a whole was very prosperous till the end of March 1914, and was in July still on a level that would have reckoned extremely high in any year prior to 1913. It is well known, however, that immediate signs of weakness were felt in the cotton trade and that a falling off there must affect perceptibly many of the totals just passed in review.

(5) THE RECORDS OF AUGUST TO DECEMBER 1914

The nature and extent of the catastrophe in August is shown very clearly in the diagrams. In spite of the inclusion of some pre-war trade the value of exported manufactures in August was only half that in January; in this category the recovery has been very slight, and the values have remained at from two-thirds to three-quarters of the monthly averages of 1906–13. The only sign of improvement is in the fact that the December total is higher than that for November, whereas in most years it has been lower. It is doubtful whether people have realized the extent of this injury to manufactures, since the monthly totals are often merged with previous months, the totals are regarded rather than the classes, and imports are frequently (and quite absurdly) added to exports. Since many people regard export of manufactures as the main purpose of international trade and measure the national industrial prosperity by its amount, and everyone must recognize its extreme importance to the populations of the manufacturing towns, it is well to bring into prominence the fact that the falling off in value has been greater than if the entire cotton export trade had ceased to exist, cotton accounting in general for more than one-third of this class; the loss of wages may be estimated as £5,000,000 a month, about one-twelfth part of the whole wages bill of the kingdom. That this loss has not been more severely felt is entirely due to the absorption of many men in the forces and another multitude in providing necessaries for the war.

The change in the value of imports of raw materials was

proportional in August, September and October to that of exported manufactures. An improvement was visible in November (which we shall find when we examine quantities instead of values greater than the tablés so far suggest), and a quite considerable rise in December; some effect may be expected in the export of manufactures in January[1], but part of the increase is no doubt due to increased military demands for wool, etc.

The relatively small values in other classes of exports will be considered in the section devoted to special commodities.

The movement of the values of imported manufactured goods has been similar to that of raw materials; since more than half of the so-called manufactures have some further process to undergo and might (with a different definition) be regarded as materials, some correlation might be expected. Actually the manufactures fell off greatly in August and September, but in December had recovered considerably and had reached the level of the same class in 1908.

At the present time the most important aspect of our external trade is the supply of food, and here the record is extraordinary. In spite of all obstacles, whether financial, or arising from lack of shipping and from hostile acts, the total value in class I (of which food and tea comprise the great part) was even in August practically equal to that in the corresponding month in 1906, '7 or '9, in September it was only less than in 1912 and 1913, and in October, November and December records were established. The value in December 1914 was 30 per cent. greater than in any previous December. A considerable part, but not all, of the increase is due to increased prices (see p. 42 below).

From the point of view of commerce the statistics of re-exports are deserving of special study; for on the one hand there must have been special inducements to citizens of neutral powers trading with each other to do without the conveniences of entrepôt furnished by London, and on the other hand, the great entrepôts of Antwerp, Rotterdam, Amsterdam and Hamburg have not been easily available. It is not easy,

---

[1] The supplementary table (p. 55) shows the January statistics.

however, to generalize from these statistics which show curious variability both monthly and annually, and it seems best only to deal with them in part in the consideration of particular commodities.

(6) THE BALANCE OF TRADE

Perhaps the most important use of the unanalyzed totals of the values of imports and exports is found in the light that the excess of imports throws on the earnings of shipping and merchanting of goods, and on the movement of capital and interest. We must now include movements of bullion and specie, as well as of goods. The following tables show the totals for the years 1901 to 1914, and also average monthly totals.

EXCESS OF IMPORTS.
£00,000s.

Year	Value of commodities	Value of bullion and specie	Total
1901	1741	∓ 62	1803
1902	1792	+ 53	1845
1903	1822	− 3	1819
1904	1800	− 7	1793
1905	1574	+ 62	1636
1906	1472	+ 18	1490
1907	1278	+ 53	1341
1908	1362	− 68	1294
1909	1552	+ 65	1617
1910	1441	+ 67	1508
1911	1233	+ 60	1293
1912	1457	+ 46	1503
1913	1339	+119	1458
1914	1717	+211	1928

EXCESS OF IMPORTS.
£00,000s.

	Value of commodities		Value of bullion and specie		Together	
	Average for 1906–13	1914	Average for 1906–13	1914	Average for 1906–13	1914
Jan. to June	700	613	+67	50	767	663
July	68	71	+13	39	81	110
August	63	137	+15	81	78	218
September	87	131	− 21	16	66	147
October	122	158	− 41	11	81	169
November	170	257	+ 9	4	179	261
December	187	354	+ 5	6	192	360

The principal causes of the permanent excess of imports, which as shown in the table has varied in recent years from £184,500,000 in 1902 to £129,300,000 in 1911, are the earnings of shipping and the receipt of other profits and interests from abroad. The former item tends to grow with the general increase in international trade, and is also subject to rather violent fluctuations with the changes of freight-charges; the latter item also grows continuously as the amount of capital invested abroad and owned by residents in the United Kingdom increases. On the other side, all exportation of capital for external investment causes an increase of exports without corresponding imports, and diminishes the excess of imports; similarly if, as is frequently the case, interests or profits payable abroad are left for re-investment, the excess of imports falls, and we may regard this process equally as an exportation of capital. Apart from years when freight-rates were abnormally high or low the changes of level in the excess for short periods are attributable to the variation of the amount of capital thus invested, a low level corresponding to much investment. After examination of all the available evidence Mr C. K. Hobson (*Export of Capital*, 1914, p. 204) estimates that in the five years 1901–1905 capital of the aggregate value of £138,000,000 was exported, while in the following six years (1906–1911) the much larger value £828,000,000 was reached; if Mr Hobson is right in his very high estimate for freight in 1912, another great exportation took place in that year, and the excess shown above for 1913 suggests that the high level continued.

Of course the transactions connected with the payments of interest, the payments of freight and the movement of goods or bullion caused by capital investment, cannot practically be identified or distinguished from each other or from the sale or purchase of goods on short credit. All go to form the great heterogeneous mass of bills which represent international transactions.

The excess for 1914 is the greatest recorded, not merely in recent years, but at any time. To it should be added the value of whatever gold has been deposited by the Bank of England in outlying parts of the empire, for in normal circumstances this would have been imported without any change of exports. From it should be subtracted the much smaller value of enemy's cargoes included in imports, for they are an unwilling gift without corresponding exports; a contrary allowance should be made for those homeward bound cargoes, belonging to residents in the United Kingdom, destroyed or captured by the enemy and paid for by home underwriters; the difference between these items is not great in comparison with the £192,800,000 in question.

The excess both of the value of commodities and of bullion varies considerably month by month. The average monthly excess of the two categories together, 1906–13, was about £120,000,000. The first half of the year accounts for rather more than half the annual average; the months July, August, September are below and October at the average, while November and December are far above it. Bullion and specie show a seasonal movement different to, and relatively more violent than, that of commodities; there is a net export in September and October in every year, 1906–13; in many years there is a net export in December and in most years in January; the net import, on the other hand, is considerable from March to August.

The alteration in 1914 is very marked. In the first seven months the excess value of imported commodities was rather less than the average (£68,400,000 against £76,800,000), and of bullion and specie was slightly greater (£8,900,000 against £8,000,000). In August the joint excess was nearly three times the average, in September and October more than twice, in November relatively not so much in excess, while in December the increase of the excess was a maximum. In the five months together the excess was £56,000,000 more than the average for the corresponding months of 1906–13, to which should be added the amount held abroad by the Bank of England. In the bullion and specie records the absence from August to December of importation of gold from South Africa is very noticeable; in these months in 1913 it was £15,210,000; in 1914, £1,725,000; nevertheless instead of exporting gold in September and October, we were importing it, while in August we had kept £6,600,000 more than usual. In addition to this £3,400,000 of gold held in London for India was released, and this is a virtual import. Further imports of commodities have been delayed by congestion at the ports, so that we ought to throw in a few days of January 1915 for comparison with former years.

A considerable part of the increase is due to the great rise in freights (including insurance); it will pass the skill of a statistician to determine how much. Another part is due to the strengthening of the gold-reserve held at home. The rest presumably is to be accounted for by the great demand for food-imports at enhanced prices, for which the customary means of payment arising from exports was checked. The balance has no doubt been met by a combination of methods, among which a check in the export of goods without immediate payment (*i.e.*, in the export of capital), and a realization of interests and profits due from abroad instead of their re-investment (a check in the virtual export of capital) have very likely been the most important. The new regulations preventing the issue of new foreign shares on the stock exchange will tend in the same direction.

Before this subject is concluded, it may be pointed out that debts due from the enemy at the declaration of war have not been collected, nor monies due to him paid. If the former were the greater, as we may reasonably expect, the excess of imports is still more remarkable. We return to the whole question on p. 53.

CHAPTER II

TRADE IN THE PRINCIPAL COMMODITIES

(1) Selection of Commodities

THERE is hardly any commodity known to man that is not both imported and exported by the traders of the United Kingdom, and in most cases the sources of imports and the destinations of exports are manifold. It is therefore extremely difficult to give a concise account of changes of trade, without concealing just those details which are important and interesting. On the whole it seems best to deal with those commodities which are of the greatest importance in aggregate value, rather than with those which happen to present special features of interest at the present time, lest the proper perspective of the mass of foreign trade should be lost.

In tabulating trade statistics we may take either countries or commodities as the main heading, and in the latter case we may measure by quantity or by value. For practical purposes of studying national needs and their satisfaction or openings for employment, *quantities* of goods imported and exported, irrespective of their value, source or destination, should have the principal place. Since we cannot add tons to gallons or scores directly, we must also deal with prices and values before we can deal with trade categories as wholes. Among the totals that are interesting to observe, especially at present, are those which relate to special countries. In this section we deal with quantities, in the next with prices and totals, and in the last with countries.

It is a characteristic of the trade of the United Kingdom, that, however it is tabulated, there is a miscellaneous residuum defying classification, and that any system rapidly becomes out of date and unsuitable, as new commodities continually become of sufficient importance to be promoted from the miscellanies to the list. In the very compact, though still voluminous, monthly accounts of trade, which are all that we can use for our present purpose, the value and quantity of all commodities, ultimately classified in the annual reports, are stated, and in a great many cases the principal countries of origin or destination are also separated; it is to these cases that we are limited, and consequently there are many important commodities that we cannot study in detail.

The tables (pp. 20, 32 *seq.*) show the changes in quantities imported and exported of all the principal commodities, comparing the amounts in 1913 and 1914, monthly from August. The units have been chosen of such a size that two or three significant figures are left in the smallest entries. Though the actual quantities for each commodity can readily be seen, the main purpose of the table is comparative, and this has determined its form. Those re-exports are included in the import table which form a considerable proportion of imports of the same kind. The values of the goods included form in the case of imported food 84 per cent. of the whole class, of imported raw materials 79 per cent., of all imports about 75 per cent. In exports are included about 50 per cent. of food, etc., 80 per cent. of raw materials, 70 per cent. of manufactures, and 70 per cent. of all. We have thus a large proportion of each trade class, and it would be only by including a very much larger number of numerically unimportant commodities that we could sensibly increase the proportion.

The selection of commodities for special analysis, in the following paragraphs, has been determined chiefly by the amount of detail as to countries of origin and destination available in the monthly reports. In recent years the method used for classifying goods by countries has been to group them according to the country from which or to which they were *consigned*. In the case of exports this is not necessarily the country in which they are used—they may be consigned to Hong-Kong and re-exported to Japan, or to Denmark and used in Germany; nor in the case of imports is the country

always that in which the goods originated or even were manufactured, but may simply be the country containing the
entrepôt port at which the goods were bought from an agent.
This consideration is more important in connection with the
near European ports than with the more distant countries
with which the trade of the last five months has chiefly taken
place. Though tabulation by countries of consignment does
not always give us the information we want for studying
industry and interchange, yet the values arrived at are very
generally precisely those appropriate for the observation of
the balance of trade between countries, since goods must
in general be paid for (directly or indirectly) at the place of
consignment.

(2) IMPORTS

(a) Food, etc.

Cereals. The total amount of *wheat* and *wheat flour* received
in 1914, including Canada's gift of 1,100,000 cwts. of flour,
and excluding re-exports, was about 3 per cent. below the
total for 1913 (7 per cent. below that for 1912, 5 per cent.
above that for 1911, a year of specially good home harvest).
In the first seven months we had been short, in spite of good
shipments from Russia, Argentina sending 7,500,000 cwts. and
India 5,900,000 cwts. less than in the first seven months of
1913; but in every month from August to December the 1914
totals were greater, and in the five months together imports
were 10 per cent. higher than in 1913.   To this increment
Canada and U.S.A. were the main contributors; the former
sent 18,700,000 cwts. of wheat in 1914 as compared with
10,800,000 cwts. in the last five months of 1913, the latter sent
4,000,000 cwts. in excess, balancing a defect in the earlier
months.   From India we received less than in 1913 in both
parts of the year. The contribution of Russia has varied greatly
in recent years, and in 1913 was unusually low; in the early
months of 1914 there was so large an increase that the total
even for the whole year was 2,200,000 cwts. up; failure of
the Black Sea trade in the autumn of 1914 has cut off part
of our supplies, and though these have been made up from

IMPORTS. *Quantities of selected commodities in 1913, 1914.*

Commodity	Unit	Jan. to July 1913	Jan. to July 1914	August 1913	August 1914	September 1913	September 1914	October 1913	October 1914	November 1913	November 1914	December 1913	December 1914	Whole year 1913	Whole year 1914
FOOD, etc.															
Wheat	100,000 cwts.	632	568	101	103	89	126	80	88	78	77	79	77	1059	1039
Wheat flour	10,000 cwts.	660	603	79	65	121	61	123	84	104	90	111	104	1198	1006
Barley	,, ,,	921	694	127	227	262	165	511	237	285	192	138	99	2244	1614
Oats	,, ,,	1259	1004	116	85	90	85	86	46	100	100	172	96	1823	1416
Maize	100,000 cwts.	248	159	53	52	60	35	68	37	37	53	26	54	492	390
Rice	10,000 cwts.	263	324	28	44	29	41	31	37	27	31	46	65	444	542
Beef	10,000 cwts.	537	584	78	72	84	37	82	61	64	64	75	67	920	884
Mutton	,, ,,	343	367	40	40	45	16	24	22	40	34	41	42	534	520
Pork	1,000 cwts.	221	469	20	23	41	82	62	100	64	94	88	93	496	861
Bacon	10,000 cwts.	284	303	42	35	38	40	42	42	37	41	43	48	486	510
Ham	1,000 cwts.	501	561	85	66	74	50	64	42	68	51	63	69	855	839
Butter	10,000 cwts.	254	260	34	24	32	25	27	30	31	27	36	33	414	398
Cheese	,, ,,	118	127	24	26	27	23	23	29	24	16	14	21	230	242
Eggs	1,200,000	1166	1202	176	72	203	68	204	121	200	165	209	163	2158	1791
Fish	1,000 cwts.	685	1052	70	64	112	111	168	143	96	117	245	140	1376	1627
Re-exported	,, ,,	311	286	35	11	43	17	57	24	43	27	46	23	470[1]	387
Lard	,, ,,	1253	1122	148	151	140	98	139	146	133	117	193	130	2005	1763
Margarine	,, ,,	855	888	119	139	136	111	129	119	129	127	150	144	1518	1629
Coffee	1,000 cwts.														
Imported	......	577	758	36	34	40	21	45	58	44	69	109	106	847	1037[1]
Entered for consumption	......	163	162	17	24	22	15	22	21	19	27	18	20	260	269
Re-exported	......	268	410	49	17	60	16	70	38	38	83	30	107	515	673

Commodity	Unit	Jan. to July 1913	Jan. to July 1914	August 1913	August 1914	September 1913	September 1914	October 1913	October 1914	November 1913	November 1914	December 1913	December 1914	Whole year 1913	Whole year 1914
Tea	100,000 lbs.														
Imported	......	1443	1578	395	392	475	393	487	203	452	491	419	716	3650	3745
Entered for consumption	......	1758	1837	247	319	261	282	286	279	271	291	246	221	3057	3175
Re-exported	......	113	108	18	9	21	25	29	84	20	60	17	18	218	305
Cocoa	100,000 lbs.	513	607	48	41	66	73	35	39	56	99	81	97	784	946
Wine	10,000 gallons	706	764	77	54	87	91	126	90	125	81	120	76	1236	1151
Sugar	10,000 cwts.														
Imported	......	2334	2230	368	72	179	166	236	409	385	644	439	556	3043	4069
Entered for consumption	......	2013	2087	312	234	268	208	248	275	303	335	319	224	3464	3364
Tobacco															
Unmanufactured	100,000 lbs,	752	783	134	120	163	128	215	181	174	188	188	203	1630	1686
Manufactured	10,000 lbs.	205	180	22	15	30	20	33	16	30	17	39	28	360	275
MATERIALS															
Iron ore	10,000 tons	472	362	53	38	53	53	60	46	53	35	54	36	744	570
Tin ore	100 tons	206	231	28	28	25	24	28	15	28	14	31	12	346	324
Cotton, raw	1,000,000 lbs.														
Imported	......	1096	1299	39	60	88	40	260	66	351	131	339	268	2174	1864
Re-exported	......	178	150	18	9	9	11	11	12	15	12	26	23	258	216
Wool, raw	100,000 lbs.														
Imported	......	6051	5467	299	265	292	293	308	121	397	249	674	720	8021	7117
Re-exported	......	1920	2697	190	240	53	49	348	38	111	3	442	25	3065	2952
Flax	100 tons	815	730	41	18	24	20	28	42	44	17	72	44	1025	871
Hemp	100 tons														
Imported	......	918	871	75	79	103	75	130	58	81	69	166	121	1463	1273
Re-exported	......	312	329	40	26	41	16	42	17	38	19	51	29	525	435

1 Especially in the case of dutiable commodities the annual totals differ slightly from the sums of the uncorrected monthly accounts. Also the total given for re-exported fish in the reports is not the sum of the monthly totals (435).

IMPORTS. *Quantities of selected commodities in 1913, 1914 (continued).*

Commodity	Unit	Jan. to July		August		September		October		November		December		Whole year	
		1913	1914	1913	1914	1913	1914	1913	1914	1913	1914	1913	1914	1913	1914
MATERIALS (*continued*)															
Jute	1,000 tons														
Imported	......	194	156	5	6	12	4	44	16	44	21	52	35	351	238
Re-exported	......	81	63	8	2	5	4	13	3	12	3	11	5	130	80
Cotton-seed	1,000 tons	391	431	25	28	25	48	52	19	57	36	62	75	615	640
Linseed	100 tons	183	151	35	28	36	31	42	13	19	13	13	10	327	245
Petroleum	1,000,000 gallons	264	375	40	38	48	52	50	62	46	66	41	54	489	647
Rubber	10,000 lbs.	926	907	113	88	131	112	138	117	135	113	131	178	1574	1515
Tallow	1,000 cwts.														
Imported	......	1132	1082	203	136	205	158	110	57	146	86	137	124	1933	1643
Re-exported	......	510	570	86	31	69	63	128	59	91	51	63	50	943	824
Paper-making materials	1,000 tons	515	505	80	52	99	171	95	115	79	72	109	75	978	990
Wood	10,000 loads	525	431	145	68	149	59	141	95	80	86	62	38	1102	777
Hides, raw	1,000 cwts.														
Imported	......	893	834	113	98	128	97	108	140	104	98	107	120	1454	1390
Re-exported	......	339	272	29	18	34	15	34	18	36	4	36	6	509	332
MANUFACTURES															
Iron and steel	1,000 tons	1278	1368	159	59	175	39	205	35	181	55	223	59	2220	1617
Copper	100 tons	624	817	98	95	85	157	100	161	80	133	83	142	1069	1505
Lead	1,000 tons	120	128	17	19	15	19	15	17	19	20	18	21	204	224
Tin	100 tons														
Imported	......	273	277	30	19	41	26	42	27	36	25	35	36	457	410
Re-exported	......	185	191	28	4	29	51	23	25	19	21	18	16	302	308

Commodity	Unit	Jan. to July		August		September		October		November		December		Whole year	
		1913	1914	1913	1914	1913	1914	1913	1914	1913	1914	1913	1914	1913	1914
Zinc	100 tons	754	667	131	62	149	135	182	124	127	64	107	105	1450	1157
Machinery	100 tons	655	702	70	34	65	20	86	36	78	42	83	53	1037	887
Cotton piece-goods	100,000 yds.	732	802	105	22	105	32	106	38	96	27	112	29	1257	950
Woollen, etc.															
Yarn	10,000 lbs.	2011	1699	250	41	262	85	304	30	237	1	235	3	3299	1859
Stuffs	10,000 yds.	3846	4057	431	82	425	200	405	95	366	37	437	47	5909	4518
Silk stuffs	100,000 yds.	626	679	93	25	99	58	95	73	86	54	93	69	1093	958
Linen															
Yarn	10,000 lbs.	1586	1411	207	51	274	240	231	425	233	52	255	5	2786	2184
Manufactures	10,000 yds.	1061	932	156	38	133	128	125	73	125	6	142	11	1741	1188
Auiline	1,000 cwts.	167	167	22	4	22	2	27	5	22	8	23	7	283	192
Painters' colours	10,000 cwts.	169	165	21	8	20	7	20	8	22	10	26	10	279	206
Leather															
Undressed	1,000 cwts.	551	546	83	66	96	26	86	56	68	151	63	188	947	1032
Dressed	,, ,,	138	127	18	6	21	6	18	29	18	33	17	32	229	234
Gloves	1000 doz. pairs	857	784	120	19	141	22	132	52	116	32	107	40	1473	948
Glass	1,000 cwts.	1648	1467	225	66	213	33	236	40	228	44	248	48	2682	1699
Paper	10,000 cwts.	741	729	113	63	109	95	119	115	98	90	109	89	1288	1181

In more detail: *Wheat flour* includes meal. *Rice* does not include meal. *Beef, Mutton, Pork* are totals of fresh, chilled and frozen but not salted or canned. *Fish* excludes fresh fish. *Sugar* is total of unrefined and refined. *Wool*, only sheep's and lamb's. *Flax* and *Hemp*, dressed and tow. *Paper-making materials*, pulp of wood only. *Wood*, hewn, sawn, planed. *Iron and steel manufactures*, all from pig-iron to steel girders, etc. *Copper*, regulus, unwrought and part wrought. *Lead*, pig and sheet. *Tin*, blocks, etc. *Zinc*, crude. *Machinery*, all kinds, including parts. *Woollen stuffs*, "other sorts," excluding some kinds especially named in import tables. *Aniline*, aniline and naphthaline dye-stuffs. *Glass*, only window, plate and flint. *Paper*, all kinds.

other sources the wheat-consuming world as a whole appears to be badly supplied till the Russian wheat is free. The home harvest of 1914 was somewhat above the average, the wheat crop being officially estimated at 62,500,000 bushels as compared with 56,700,000 in 1913; and allowing for this it is clear that our supply in 1914 was adequate, and that the present high prices cannot be attributed to any shortage manifested in 1914.

The importation of both *barley* and *oats* has fallen short; the defect in the former is mainly attributable to India and to Turkey, of the latter to Russia, Germany and Argentina.

Maize has been short for want of 10,000,000 cwts. from Argentina, whose shipments in 1913 were unusually great; a deficit from U.S.A. was balanced by an excess from Roumania.

The proportions of the crops named contributed by different countries vary greatly from year to year[1], and there was nothing exceptional in the sources of supply in 1914.

Meat. The supply of *beef* from Argentina was nearly normal before the war, and the less important supply from Australia and New Zealand in excess of the normal. By the end of the year, however, we were nearly 1,000,000 cwts. short from Argentina, September being the worst month, while the receipts in December were only 62 per cent. of those in December 1913. From Australia and New Zealand big shipments arriving in August and December compensated smaller loads in September, October and November. In all, the shortage in the five months was as much as 22 per cent. of the 1913 supply, unless there were direct shipments to our troops on the continent.

In the case of the normal supply of *mutton* the proportions contributed by Argentina and Australasia respectively are the reverse of those for beef. The Argentine supply was in excess throughout the year, except for September and December. The Australasian supply was short from August to November. In all the shortage in the supply of mutton in the last five months was 19 per cent. of the 1913 supply, nearly as serious as in the case of beef. It remains to be seen how far this supply is merely delayed, and how far the deficit is absolute.

[1] See the *Statistical Abstract for the United Kingdom* for 1913, Table 44.

The extra 100,000 cwts. of *pork* imported since July, mainly from the Netherlands, would not go far to make up for the absence of beef and mutton, even if it were not balanced by a diminution of *ham*.

We were as much as 13 per cent. short in imported *butter* from August to December, and this is accounted for by the small supplies from Russia in August and September. Sweden has also sent less than usual, but France has supplied that deficit. There has been little exceptional in the *cheese* supply.

Russia supplied one-half and Denmark one-fifth of our imported *eggs* in 1912 and 1913. Denmark has done better than usual, but 70 per cent. of the Russian supply has been lost in the last five months, a shortage of about 500,000,000 eggs.

Dutiable goods, of which the most important for our purpose are tea and sugar, are counted as imports at the time they are landed, but are in general warehoused under bond; when they are needed for current supplies the duty is paid and they are withdrawn; at this time they are "entered for home consumption[1]" in the customs house accounts. The amount withdrawn from the bonded warehouses in any month has no necessary relation to the amount imported in that month.

The amount of *tea* imported was much as usual in 1914, a slight excess being balanced by re-export. The autumn deliveries both from China and India were delayed, and only after the *Emden* was accounted for was the usual total made up. Meanwhile the stock was sufficient for the ordinary withdrawals for consumption. As regards re-exports, Russia received (in direct consignment from England at any rate), 7,000,000 lbs. less in 1914 than in 1913, while "other European countries" took 19,000,000 lbs. more; presumably this tea came into London instead of into a continental port. Canada also had an excess from England of 3,700,000 lbs.

To get a complete statement for *sugar* we must depend on future reports of the Royal Commission which has it in charge. The supply and consumption of the first seven months of 1914 was nearly normal; in the last five months, 15 per cent.

---

[1] The alternative is that they should be withdrawn for re-export.

more than usual was imported, 13 per cent. less than usual was taken for consumption, and re-exports were not significant; the visible supply has increased by 5,600,000 cwts. in the period. After a small importation in August the usual supply was nearly reached in September and greatly exceeded in subsequent months. The following table shows how greatly the sources of supply have changed.

IMPORTS *of sugar, August to December.*

00,000 cwts.

				1913	1914
Germany	..	..	..	86	1
Austria ..	..	..	..	26	1
Netherlands	..	..	..	17	8
Belgium	..	..	..	5	—
Cuba ..	..	..	..	9	10
Mauritius	..	..	..	1	6
W. Indies	..	..	..	2	9
Java ..	..	..	..	—	62
Other countries		..	..	15	87
Total ..	..	..		161	184

The "other countries" which have, together with Java, given the bulk of the increase have not hitherto been important enough to be separately enumerated in the monthly accounts, and we are therefore in ignorance as to their names. The increase is mainly in refined sugar, and it is known that U.S.A. has contributed.

The remaining commodities in the first part of the table (pp. 20–1) call for no special comment. There has been no evident serious difficulty in the food supply.

(b) Raw materials

Iron-ore, of which about two-thirds comes from Spain, was imported in only three-quarters of its 1913 amount, both in the first seven and last five months of 1914. *Tin-ore* has been short during the last three months. Unwrought tin, classed under manufactures, was imported in smaller quantities than usual from August to November, though re-exports were normal.

The importation of *cotton* was up to July considerably

greater than in 1913, the United States, Egypt and India, each sending more than usual. In August, a month in which relatively little is due, the States' consignment was up to that of the previous year while India's was well in excess. In September again little is due, but less even than usual came from the States. The importation in October and November should be considerable, but we only got 164 instead of 483 million lbs. from the States, and 16 instead of 92 from Egypt. There was a considerable improvement in December; rather more than usual was received from Egypt and India, while 196 instead of 264 million lbs. arrived from the States. In January 1915 the deliveries were 300 million lbs., as compared with 307 in January 1914.

Relatively little wool (sheep's and lamb's) is delivered from May to November; the supply was nearly normal in August and September, and the diminution of imports in October and November was balanced, so far as home manufactures were concerned, by lessened re-exports. December's imports were above normal, and owing to the virtual absence of re-exports the home-supply was considerably increased. The total imports, less re-exports, in the first seven months of 1914 was 126 million lbs. less than 1913, in the last five months 46 million lbs. greater. Germany secured her usual annual amount of colonial wool from London, with remarkable foresight, before the declaration of war, and 5 million lbs. of wool was cleared to Germany after the July trade accounts were closed. The December deliveries from S. Africa were short, those from Argentina in excess.

In January 1915 104 million lbs. were received, as compared with 101 in January 1914.

Alpaca wool, of which almost the only source is Peru, came in very small quantities from September to the end of the year, probably because of the neighbourhood of the German squadron till December. *Mohair*, for the supply of which we depend mainly on South Africa and secondarily on Turkey, was in defect from September to November; the December amount was above the level, owing to the receipt of delayed supplies from Africa.

Except for the Turkish mohair the sources of supply of cotton and wool are not directly affected by the war, and, since the principal continental purchasers have taken less than usual, the quantities available for the United Kingdom should be ample.

The position as to *flax* is not so satisfactory, for the main source of supply is Russia, and the next most important is Belgium, Holland being third after a great interval. There had been a considerable falling off before the end of July and the importation from August to October is generally small; but owing to a considerable delivery from Belgium in October (despatched, no doubt, before the investment of Antwerp) the receipts were only 13 per cent. short in these months. Holland has sent more than usual, but in November and December the difficulties in the way of the Russian supply had great effect, and there seems no way of obtaining it except at a prohibitive cost till the Baltic is open. As is well known, Belfast depends to an enormous extent on foreign supplies both of flax and yarn, and the latter is also difficult to obtain. The Russian 1914 crop is only now due; most of that from Belgium of 1913 is to hand and in process of manufacture. If the Belgian crop of 1914 has been destroyed, there must be a dearth of the flax suitable for fine linen within the year.

The *hemp* supply has been irregular, the deliveries from the Philippines, the main source, were only three-tenths and four-tenths of the 1913 amounts in October and December, presumably owing to the menace of the *Emden*; the November supply equalled the very small amount of November, 1913. Part of the deficit through the autumn was made up by Italy. New Zealand, India and Russia are the other sources. There seems no reason why an adequate supply should not be available in the near future.

For *jute* we depend almost entirely on India. The delivery has been delayed, but it will presumably soon take place, and the diminution of re-export should afford an ample supply for Dundee's needs.

The only serious problem in the supply of textile fibres

is then in connection with flax, which can of course for many purposes be replaced by cotton and for others by jute.

Oil seeds (castor, cotton, flax, rape, soya-beans, etc.), *seed oil,* and *oil-seed cake* are imported from many countries, and exported or re-exported; their main use is for food for cattle. Of these linseed has been the most important, the main supply coming from India, Canada, Argentina and Russia, though the contributions of these countries seem very variable. Actually more was received from Russia and India in 1914 than in 1913, but the Canadian supply (which had been negligible in 1912 but great in 1913) was quite small in 1914. Other seeds were normal; but cotton-seed cake and linseed oil and cake were short. On the whole there has been a serious shortage in this group.

The importation of *petroleum*, which has been on the increase for several years, was in 1914 much greater than before. In 1913 we had obtained three-fifths of our supply from U.S.A., and one-fifth from Russia or Roumania; no details are available for 1914.

The supply of *rubber* has been well maintained from all its ordinary sources.

Of *tallow* the Australian, Argentine and Chinese shipments have been short.

The alarm felt in August from the small mass of the available stock of *paper-making materials* was short-lived; large deliveries were obtained in September, and though the proportions from the numerous countries, which supply the material in various forms, have altered, the total in the last five months of 1914 was greater than in the corresponding period of 1913.

With *wood* the difficulty has been more serious. The importation prior to the war was a fifth less than in 1913, and (except for a recovery in November) has been worse from August to December. The failure of the Russian supply has not as yet been compensated by increase from other countries.

Hides and *leather* (which is classed as manufactured) may be considered together. In the last five months of 1914 the weight of hides, wet or dry, and leather, undressed or dressed, imported and not re-exported, was about 980,000 cwts. as compared with 710,000 cwts. in 1913. The sources of supply are numerous. The available supply of hides has increased owing to the falling of re-export and that of leather, owing to increased shipments from U.S.A. and to diminished re-export. The supply of sheep and goat-skins, when imports, exports and re-exports are considered together, is found to be slightly greater in 1914 than in 1913.

(c) *Manufactures*

Under *iron* and *steel* were included in 1913 £1,000,000 worth of pig-iron, £2,600,000 worth of steel "blooms, billets and slabs," and £12,600,000 worth of material in a more developed state of manufacture, such as bars, sheets, girders and rails. The average value of all was about £7 per ton. In the last five months of 1914 we were about 700,000 tons short.

So-called manufactured *copper* and *lead* is simply unwrought or wrought metal; the latter has been normal, the former has arrived in considerably increased quantities. The supply of *zinc* has fallen short.

The sources of importation of *machinery*, of textile *yarns* and *stuffs*, of *gloves* and of *glass* are to a very great extent the countries now at war. In each case the deliveries have fallen off very greatly, as can be seen from the table, p. 22. The monthly reports do not distinguish countries of origin, so the causes cannot be analyzed; but no doubt our receipts of silk and of woollen stuffs from France have been much smaller than usual and we have lacked the usual supply of German glass.

Taking a general view of imports, it may be said that there are few necessary commodities, usually imported on a large scale, whose supply has been seriously disorganized. In spite of delays in transport, accentuated by the congestion at the docks of London and Liverpool, in December and January, such goods were being obtained in nearly every case in sufficient quantities by the end of the year, and large supplies are afloat or ready for shipment. This result has been attained either by drawing on "other countries" (an elusive category, now of special interest), or by keeping at home consignments which would normally have been re-exported, or by developing manufacture for home at the expense of foreign use. Since the home supply of raw materials is relatively unimportant, the statistics of imports, of re-exports, and of exports of home produce are generally sufficient to allow a judgment to be formed.

While most of the manufactured goods usually imported, can be replaced by English made goods, the transference and adaptation takes time; in the case of drugs and of dye-stuffs, almost new industries have to be created and new processes developed, unless substitutes can be found. There are also many cheap German products, which will hardly pay the cost of manufacture, and which can readily be dispensed with. Some specialized productions, e.g., of scientific instruments, are difficult to replace at home, and the alleged failure of the supply of potash, and doubtless of other things which do not figure largely in the trade accounts, may give trouble. We have still, moreover, to complete twelve months of disturbance, and the disorganization of interchange in the spring may reveal further inconveniences; but the frame-work of modern trade and manufacture is wonderfully elastic and adaptable, and so far as one can judge any effects that are felt will be rather in enhanced price than in absence of supply.

(3) EXPORTS

(a) *Food, tobacco, materials*

In exported food *herrings* are the only commodity of importance. June to December are the principal months, and, of these, November accounts for a great proportion. Germany took half and Russia one-third of the total in 1913. Russia obtained small quantities till October, but the trade has all but been destroyed for the season. The fear of depletion of the supply, that has been prevalent for some time, will be removed after the herrings' Sabbatical year.

EXPORTS of home produce. Quantities of selected commodities, 1913-1914.

Commodity [1]	Unit	Jan. to July		August		September		October		November		December		Whole year	
		1913	1914	1913	1914	1913	1914	1913	1914	1913	1914	1913	1914	1913	1914
Fish, cured............	10,000 cwts.	252	304	112	31	132	39	102	38	220	29	134	18	953	458
Beer............	1,000 barrels	378	369	44	30	53	40	59	32	58	36	63	31	656	539
Spirits............	10,000 gallons	564	626	78	87	92	92	86	77	98	71	90	57	1009	1010
Tobacco............	100,000 lbs.	177	226	31	23	31	23	31	28	33	22	27	27	330	349
Coal............	100,000 tons	425	412	58	31	62	39	67	39	59	33	62	37	734	590
Wool............	100,000 lbs.	155	288	22	34	22	31	32	25	26	4	32	2	287	385
Seed oil............	100 tons	341	324	48	25	44	29	54	37	51	50	50	54	587	520
MANUFACTURES															
Iron and steel........	1,000 tons	2950	2750	388	204	386	225	426	261	420	237	366	210	4934	3889
Copper............	10 tons	3041	2990	361	226	418	105	475	264	649	216	378	208	5321	4009
Tin............	100 tons	73	71	9	7	7	8	9	12	9	15	7	20	115	134
Cutlery............	100 cwts.	295	267	42	23	41	32	51	27	40	23	34	21	503	391
Hardware............	1,000 cwts.	621	588	82	48	84	47	88	45	82	38	81	36	1038	803
Machinery............	1,000 tons	436	444	59	32	62	30	67	35	66	33	57	26	747	601
Cotton															
Waste............	100,000 lbs.	630	591	90	24	68	12	117	15	92	21	109	36	1107	700
Yarn............	100,000 lbs.	1230	1333	160	81	157	97	200	80	182	95	172	100	2101	1785
Piece............	10,000,000 yds.	422	409	58	31	55	37	63	37	56	31	55	27	707	573
Flags, etc............	100,000 yds.	432	509	61	36	68	26	73	30	69	27	68	29	772	658

[1] Iron and steel manufactures—pig-iron, steel, iron and steel girders, etc., wire, etc. Copper—unwrought, yellow, wrought, manufacture. Tin—unwrought. Flags, etc.—goods not in the piece. Wool, yarn—wool, worsted, alpaca, mohair, etc. Sulphate—of ammonia. Leather—not gloves, boots, or belting. Earthenware—china, porcelain, earthenware and pottery.

Commodity	Unit	Jan. to July 1913	Jan. to July 1914	August 1913	August 1914	September 1913	September 1914	October 1913	October 1914	November 1913	November 1914	December 1913	December 1914	Whole year 1913	Whole year 1914
Wool and worsted															
Tops	10,000 lbs.	2612	3105	370	180	330	172	387	150	369	30	296	48	4363	3686
Yarn	10,000 lbs.	4813	4718	578	280	662	109	709	119	656	59	624	61	8041	5348
Woollen tissues	100,000 yds.	620	597	114	60	86	45	73	35	77	33	90	52	1059	822
Worsted tissues	100,000 yds.	384	469	51	54	42	46	40	50	44	43	64	42	625	704
Carpets	10,000 sq. yds.	519	461	80	50	66	50	65	36	59	41	72	39	860	677
Silk stuffs	10,000 yds.	658	673	113	62	109	70	104	69	90	72	101	76	1184	1022
Jute															
Yarn	100,000 lbs.	262	271	28	12	36	13	33	13	30	21	31	18	418	348
Piece	100,000 yds.	997	894	136	69	164	128	160	105	145	96	143	55	1734	1347
Linen															
Yarn	10,000 lbs.	996	975	124	54	120	49	141	58	136	52	116	58	1631	1246
Piece	100,000 yds.	1193	1128	118	91	112	168	175	149	144	125	195	128	1937	1789
Boots	1,000 doz. pairs	977	995	148	130	162	145	162	151	136	104	136	164	1720	1688
Hats	1,000 dozen	958	867	138	102	109	75	102	68	96	57	115	59	1519	1229
Sulphate	1,000 tons	187	190	23	19	28	26	31	26	27	25	29	28	323	314
Other manures	1,000 tons	198	203	45	23	42	30	38	32	33	14	25	24	381	327
Painter's colours	10,000 cwts.	145	144	20	13	19	14	21	15	20	13	21	13	246	212
Soda compounds	10,000 cwts.	422	395	70	35	64	68	74	88	49	65	50	68	727	719
Leather	1,000 cwts.	139	186	20	11	21	10	27	7	25	4	24	4	256	222
Earthenware	10,000 cwts.	242	217	33	21	31	19	33	23	34	20	30	18	404	318
Paper	10,000 cwts.	210	198	28	22	29	22	29	25	27	24	26	21	351	313

The diminution of the export of *beer* and of *spirits*, which go mainly to the colonies and dominions, has not been serious. The trade in *tobacco*, of which China, the Straits and India take the bulk, has been normal.

Coal is exported in large quantities to all the maritime countries of Europe and to Argentina. The cessation of trade with Germany, Belgium and Russia accounts for the great part of the decrease; but Italy, Egypt, Spain and Argentina have taken less than usual.

The increased exportation of *wool* in 1914 is entirely attributable to large shipments to the United States before August. In August and September a further export to the States balanced the falling off to Germany and Russia; France took 1,000,000 lbs. in October, and nearly all the rest of the wool available remained at home in November and December.

These few paragraphs have dealt with all that is essential in exports other than manufactures.

(b)   *Manufactures*

Metal products. In the latter months of 1913 we sent considerable quantities of *pig-iron* to Germany, France and Belgium; in August to December 1914 we had from the absence of this trade 150,000 tons available for home use, and failure of export to other countries provided a further nearly equal amount. This accounts for the falling-off of the importation of iron-ore from Spain, mentioned above. More advanced products of iron are exported to many countries in small quantities and to India on a big scale. The shipments to most countries have been greatly diminished, with little recovery since August, except to France who took an unusual supply in December.

The exports of *cutlery* and of *hardware* have suffered, not only from lack of trade with Germany, but also from a great diminution of consignments to Brazil, Argentina, Chile, Canada and "other countries."

Machinery is entered in so many classes that generalization is difficult. It is noticeable that railway locomotives have been more in demand in both parts of 1914 than in 1913, principally from the needs of India; the total value in 1914 was £3,800,000, as compared with £2,800,000 in the former year. Agricultural self-moving machinery showed a deficiency of only £200,000 from the total (£1,360,000) of 1913, but in the first part of the year there had been a considerable increase; South America is responsible for more than half ot t̆e fall, countries in Europe for the rest.

The exports of other self-moving machinery were valued at £4,500,000 in 1913, £3,800,000 in 1914. The first part of the year had shown a growth. Many European countries took smaller consignments than usual in the autumn. Taking "Prime Movers" (including locomotives) in the aggregate, we find the value of exports was £10,000,000 approximately in both 1913 and 1914.

Other machinery (excluding electrical) was exported to the value of £24,800,000 in 1913, but only of £19,200,000 in 1914, though the first seven months had shown little change. Half the fall is to be attributed to textile machinery. Our chief customers are (in order) India, Russia, Japan, Germany and France; these, together with South American and other countries, all received greatly diminished supplies. The deficiency in non-textile machinery is to be attributed to Europe and South America in not very unequal proportions.

Textile manufactures. The history of the *cotton* industry in 1914 is very complicated[1]. Before the declaration of the war, the principal markets were overstocked, and it was already arranged to work short time for three months. The temporary failure of credit, on which the cotton manufacture (with its elaborate system of dealing in futures and of distributing risks) depends more than other industries, made trade almost impossible in August and September. Difficulties were increased by a great fall in price of raw cotton, where

---

[1] It is dealt with in great detail, in a very illuminating and instructive manner by Professor S. J. Chapman and Mr D. Kemp in a paper read to the Royal Statistical Society on January 19th, 1915, and to be published in the Society's Journal in March. The paragraph in the text summarizes part of the paper.

an unusually good harvest coincided with a contracted demand;
spinners, weavers and merchants were unwilling to proceed
till they had some guarantee that their goods would not
lose value before they were sold. The belligerent countries
(especially Germany) are important purchasers of yarn, but
not of piece-goods. India and other eastern countries take
also great quantities of yarn, as well as an enormous share
of piece-goods[1]. By the end of the year the difficulties connected with credit and with price seem to have been removed;
as we have seen, raw cotton was imported in fairly large
quantities in December. The cotton trade looks forward to
fairly good business in the near future. The depressing
statistics on p. 32 for 1914 must not, then, be regarded as
forecasting further trouble in Lancashire. (See p. 55.)

The following table shows the relative importance of
different branches of the *woollen* industry, so far as international trade is concerned.

	Value in £00,000s.			
	1913		1914	
	Imports	Exports	Imports	Exports
Raw wool, hair, waste, etc.	31	46	34	44
Manufactures				
Tops[2]	—	37	—	32
Yarn	35	80	21	55
Woollen tissues	53	{ 145 }	44	{ 116
Worsted ,, ...		{ 62 }		{ 62
Carpets	7	15	5	13
Hosiery (of wool)	5	20	4	18
Other manufactures	5	18	2	19
Total manufactures ...	105	377	76	315

Germany is the principal customer for both *tops* and
yarn; the trade in these with other manufacturing countries
also fell off greatly from the commencement of the war.
The importation of yarn practically ceased.

---

[1] In 1913 the value of exported yarn was £15,000,000, of piece-goods
£98,000,000; in 1914 the value of exported yarn was £12,000,000, of piece-
goods £79,000,000.

[2] "Tops" is the trade name for worsted after it is combed and before it
is spun.

Though most classes of manufactured wool are both imported and exported, there are considerable differences in kind between the sales and the purchases, so that the spinners and weavers of Yorkshire cannot automatically make good the absence of foreign supply; nevertheless, with some adaptation of machinery and substitution of kinds and qualities, the ordinary home demand can be met.

The trade in *woollen tissues* up to July was good, though not up to the level of 1913; the eastern markets, Argentina, Canada, Belgium and France had been weak; Germany, Holland and Australia normal; a large trade with U.S.A. had saved the situation. From August onwards the export was only half that of 1913; Australia and U.S.A. alone made purchases up to the normal, the latter considerably in excess of 1913. In December France took £460,000 worth (nearly 2,000,000 yards).

Owing to enormously increased shipments to U.S.A. (which continued throughout the year) the trade in *worsted tissues* before August was very good and continued good till November. European purchases of worsted are not very important. The relative failure in December is attributable to small eastern trade, and especially to Australia who had taken considerably more than usual up to September.

The West Riding has thus preserved the major part of its export trade, it has the deficiency of imports to make up, and the home-market (which is held to be at least as important as the foreign market to the wool industry) has been greatly stimulated by the needs of the army, though probably ordinary purchases have diminished. No doubt individual firms have difficulties, but it appears that the industrial population as a whole has quite as much to do as it can manage.

Jute manufactures are exported principally to U.S.A. and to Canada; trade to both countries had fallen back from the high level of 1913 before August, and has been (as the table on p. 33 shows) considerably curtailed ever since. The industry is not, however, very seriously depressed.

Exports of *linen* piece-goods have been fairly well maintained, except in December, in spite of the failure of supply of flax. U.S.A. and Australia are the best customers, followed by Canada and India. The December fall is attributable to smaller purchases by U.S.A.

The stoppage of imports of Belgian *yarn* since October will of course help to keep spinners busy if the raw material can be obtained; meanwhile Germany, Belgium and France, who normally take two-fifths of the yarn exported, have ceased to purchase; the remainder of the trade has suffered little.

The trade in *boots* and *shoes* with most countries has been fairly good; the loss of trade with Germany and Belgium, and some slackening with other countries, has been nearly compensated by the sale of 1,000,000 pairs (£648,000) to France.

The other manufactures enumerated in the table may be taken as illustrations of miscellaneous exports, which are too varied and numerous to deal with briefly.

It is very difficult to summarize the details found in the foregoing analysis, since the effect of the war has varied greatly from industry to industry. The first half of 1914 had differed from 1913 in many important respects; trade with Canada was bad; various eastern countries and Argentina were not normal; the goodness of aggregate trade came from a balance of improvement and deterioration. It is quite evident, however, that the disturbance has not been confined to trade with Europe, nor to trade in any one commodity. The analysis will be more definite when we summarize by countries and not by commodities, in the last chapter.

CHAPTER III

AGGREGATE QUANTITIES AND PRICES

(1) METHOD

IT is easily seen from a preliminary study of the statistics that the value of part of the trade of the past few months has been inflated by increased prices, and it is common knowledge that some prices have risen considerably. In order to compare recent with previous trade it is necessary to eliminate the effect of the variation of prices. To carry out this process the average prices (obtained by dividing the value of the imported and exported goods by their quantity or weight) for the first half of 1914 were ascertained for each of the commodities enumerated in the tables, pp. 20 and 32 *seq.*, with more detail for machinery than is there given. The quantities of goods in the first half of 1913 and in each month of the latter halves of 1913 and 1914 were re-valued at these fixed prices, and the values so obtained were totalled for each of the three main classes of imports and exports. As stated above the commodities so dealt with account for 70 or 80 per cent. of the value of all commodities. The residues are dealt with by proportion, thus: the value of the principal articles of food imported in December 1914 was £28,200,000, whereas at the prices of January to June 1914 it would have been £22,500,000, *i.e.*, 21 per cent. less; the value of all articles of food imported was £34,400,000, and, if we assume that the same percentage should be subtracted for the total as for the major part, we find by taking off 21 per cent. that the value at the fixed prices would have been £27,200,000. This method is used throughout, and is indeed that universally employed for this problem; unless very exceptional price movements have taken place in considerable parts of the residue, very little error can be introduced.

A second source of possible error may be found in the wideness of the categories used. Thus all woollen tissues are in this calculation taken together[1]; but it might have happened that the export of the less expensive kinds had diminished more than that of the more expensive, so that the average price of all would have risen though the prices of similar cloth were steady; in that case our method would have over-corrected the effect of price. Unless there has been a general movement of this kind in several important commodities and all in the same direction, the effect of this ambiguity must be quite small. We may in fact accept the results of the computation as measuring values at fixed prices within perhaps 2 per cent.

(2) Change in Quantity of Trade

The table on p. 42 shows the main results. The values for the separate months of 1913 have also been worked out, and are used in the following paragraphs, but are not given in the table. The most significant differences are in imported food and materials. In the case of *food* the whole value in 1914 was 3 per cent. more than that in 1913, but if there had been no change in price it would have been $5\frac{1}{2}$ per cent. less; that is, the imported supply of food was in quantity $5\frac{1}{2}$[2] per cent. smaller in 1914 than in 1913. The supply till the end of June was practically the same in the two years, while the July quantity was 8 per cent. short. In August, September and October we obtained only six-sevenths of the 1913 quantity though it cost $\frac{24}{25}$ths of the 1913 amount, September being the

---

[1] Lack of time alone prevents the separation into broad and narrow, heavy and light, in this case; in the *Economist's* and Board of Trade's annual calculations this is no doubt done. It is very unlikely that any significant difference would appear in the general totals, if further detail were used.

[2] This excludes Canadian and other gifts; including it we should say 5 per cent. The aggregate flour, oats, cheese, salmon, potatoes and sugar sent would have been worth about £1,000,000 at the prices of November 1914.

worst month; in November and December we obtained respectively 5 and 7 per cent. more than in the previous year. In making the comparison it must be remembered that supplies are delayed; 16 days' imports in January would be enough to complete the 1914 external supply of food up to the level of 1913.

With *materials* the price movement has in the aggregate been in the opposite direction, and we have imported more than appears from the statistics of value. The totals from January to July in 1913 and 1914 were equal; in August to November, the percentages that 1914 quantities formed of 1913 quantities were 79, 71, 51 and 59 respectively; in December it had risen to 86. If we eliminated cotton, the numbers would be 70, 77, 69, 82 and 93 per cent. respectively for the five months. The deficiency in materials has thus been considerable, and even if the importation becomes normal in 1915, there will remain the loss of last autumn's trade.

In imported *manufactures* the effect of price variations is very small and hardly beyond the possible error of the calculation.

With imports as a whole we find of course the result of the appreciation of food modified by the depreciation of materials and by the stationariness of other commodities. The aggregate value of imports was 10 per cent. lower in 1914 than in 1913; if prices had been unchanged (lower in both years than in January to June 1914) the value would have been 11 per cent. lower. It is curious that the effect of the high price of food at the end of 1914 should be so completely masked.

In exports the changes in price have been trifling in most of the commodities which bulk largely. With materials and manufactures prices were slightly higher in 1913 than in the first half of 1914, and they fell again in September 1914, recovering by the end of the year. The general result is that the value of aggregate exports of home produce in 1914 was 18 per cent. less than in 1913, while if prices had not changed the deficit would have been 17½ per cent., an insignificant difference.

Change of Quantity of Trade.

Actual values of Imports and Exports and values computed at unchanged prices.

(Average price Jan. to June 1914, taken as standard.) £00,000.

| | 1913 | 1914 | | | | | | |
| | | Jan. to | | | | | | |
Imports	Total	June	July	Aug.	Sept.	Oct.	Nov.	Dec.	Total
Food, etc.									
Actual value	2908	1359	242	215	230	281	314	344	2985
Value at fixed prices	2902	1359	243	199	201	224	245	274	2745
Materials									
Actual value	2819	1393	187	139	144	138	150	213	2364
Value at fixed prices	2748	1393	191	139	139	141	160	244	2407
Manufactures									
Actual value	1936	990	163	68	76	96	94	117	1604
Value at fixed prices	1895	990	161	66	76	96	96	118	1603
All (including miscellaneous)									
Actual value	7694	3760	594	424	451	516	560	675	6980
Value at fixed prices	7586	3760	598	406	418	463	503	638	6786

Exports (Home Produce)									
Food, etc.									
Actual value	327	144	27	15	22	22	20	19	269
Value at fixed prices	340	144	36	16	21	22	19	19	277
Materials (Coal, etc.)									
Actual value	699	341	62	29	35	37	30	33	567
Value at fixed prices	691	341	62	30	37	38	31	34	573
Manufactures									
Actual value	4115	2016	347	194	207	224	191	203	3382
Value at fixed prices	4092	2016	348	190	213	230	195	196	3388
All (including miscellaneous)									
Actual value	5254	2555	444	242	267	286	246	263	4303
Value at fixed prices	5228	2555	448	239	275	294	251	257	4319

Shipping Statistics.

Tonnage of ships entered and cleared with cargoes from and to various countries.

(tons 10,000s).

Entered	4906	2345	457	323	273	317	301	299	4315
Cleared	6782	3320	631	247	363	383	312	344	5600

(3) Shipping

An alternative, but less definite, measure of quantity of trade is found in the shipping statistics. In the table opposite is shown the aggregate tonnage of the ships which brought imports ("entered with cargoes") or took exports ("cleared"). The tonnage of ships is not in strict proportion to their carrying capacity, nor were all ships loaded completely and solely with cargoes for the United Kingdom or from it, for many call to load or discharge only part of their cargo, in which case the whole tonnage is still counted. Also the measure by cubic content, which tonnage statistics tend to give, is essentially different from the measure by fixed value used above. The relations between all these variables are likely to be fairly constant in normal years (unless the definition of tonnage, etc., changes), but are certain to have altered considerably in the exceptional trade of 1914. We find, however, a closer relation between the two parts of the table, than the obvious one that the greater is the trade the greater the shipping that carries it. Expressing all the numbers concerned as percentages of the aggregates in 1913, we have:

	1913		1914		1913		1914	
	Imports at fixed prices	Shipping entered	Imports at fixed prices	Shipping entered	Exports at fixed prices	Shipping cleared	Exports at fixed prices	Shipping cleared
Jan. to July	57·4	56·2	57·4	57·2	57·8	57·2	57·4	58·4
August	7·3	8·6	5·4	6·6	8·4	8·5	4·6	3·6
September .	8·0	9·4	5·5	5·6	8·1	8·6	5·2	5·4
October	9·3	9·2	6·0	6·5	8·9	9·2	5·6	5·7
November .	8·8	8·0	6·6	6·2	8·6	8·3	4·8	4·6
December ..	9·2	8·6	8·4	6·1	8·2	8·2	4·9	5·1
	100	100	89·3	88·4	100	100	82·6	82·8

Almost the only significant difference between tonnage and quantity is in the case of imports in December 1914; either the cargoes were intrinsically more valuable, or the ships were more completely loaded than in other months, or (as is known to have happened) a larger proportion of the cargoes was discharged in English ports and less taken on to the continent. It may be noticed that the value of imports carried per ton of entrances is much greater than the value of home produce carried per ton of clearances; the bulkiness of coal, a principal export, accounts for this.

(4) Prices

Wholesale prices can of course be deduced from these statistics, but it must be remembered that their movements measure the changes, not of quite definite and uniform commodities, but of the aggregates of goods put in the same category in the abridged table used.   Thus the rise in price of wood or of fish may be due in part to superior kinds being imported or exported.   As already argued, such changes are unlikely to affect whole classes or the general index-numbers, and in several cases the nature of the commodities is practically constant.   The table opposite shows the price-movements of those commodities which form considerable parts of imports or of exports.

The table needs little comment, though its details are very interesting and important.   In imports, of course, the prices include the cost at the place of origin, the freight and insurance[1], while exports are unaffected (except quite indirectly) by the last two.   Exports in fact show few large price movements, the main exceptions being cotton-yarn and leather; whereas the former has cheapened as the result of cheap imports of cotton, the latter has risen greatly in spite of the stationariness of the price of imported hides.   No doubt there are many factors which determine the price of leather, but it would be interesting to know whether the first impression, that the holders of the raw material are making great profits, would be confirmed by detailed investigation.   In the table leather does not include boots nor gloves.   It is satisfactory that exports on the whole have not decreased in price in spite of the curtailment of the effective demand.

Sugar (where the proportion of different qualities has changed) heads the list of increases in price of food, followed by beef, wheat and mutton.   The great part of the rise in the price of wheat is subsequent to October.   Butter rose

---

[1] But not the duties.

WHOLESALE PRICES OF SELECTED COMMODITIES.

Average, January to June 1914 = 100.

	Average 1913	Average Jan. to June 1914	July 1914	Average Aug. to Oct. 1914	Nov. 1914	Dec. 1914
Imported						
Wheat	103	100	102	109	124	130
Maize	100	100	101	115	108	111
Beef	98	100	102	131	142	145
Mutton	98	100	103	114	122	121
Bacon...............	105	100	99	116	105	108
Butter	100	100	98	109	111	117
Tea..................	101	100	98	101	106	105
Sugar	103	100	105	200	192	188
Iron-ore	104	100	99	100	99	99
Raw cotton	104	100	101	81	68	71
„ wool	99	100	102	108	108	102
„ jute	89	100	83	86	79	72
Linseed	97	100	107	107	106	107
Petroleum	106	100	89	96	83	79
Rubber	124	100	93	97	103	98
Paper materials	102	100	88	115	122	121
Wood	105	100	102	114	121	117
Hides	95	100	102	103	94	102
Exported						
Fish	90	100	77	97	119	135
Spirits	108	100	97	107	105	110
Tobacco	94	100	89	97	94	90
Coal	101	100	99	96	96	98
Iron and steel manufactures	104	100	103	104	103	106
Machinery	98	100	98	103	97	102
Cotton: Yarn	102	100	99	88	76	74
Piece goods	100	100	99	98	98	101
Wool: Yarn	98	100	100	110	116	111
Woollens	96	100	102	94	80	110
Worsteds	111	100	110	92	94	96
Linen piece..........	103	100	100	104	112	110
Jute piece	92	100	98	93	96	106
Sulphate	105	100	88	86	86	87
Leather	111	100	115	107	157	158
Paper	102	100	100	100	93	97
Aggregates[1]						
Imports: Food	100	100	100	116	128	125
Materials	103	100	98	100	94	87
All	101	100	99	109	112	107
Exports: Manufactures	101	100	100	97	98	104
All	100	100	99	98	98	102
Sauerbeck's Index-No.	103	100	100	108	107	111

[1] These depend on many more items than are given in this table.

by the end of the year, but tea (excluding the duty) and bacon were little higher than in 1913. Imported food in the lump rose 25 per cent. by the end of the year, but this must not be interpreted as meaning that retail food prices rose by just that amount, for the commodities consumed are not in the same proportion as those imported (since the home supply affects this) and the relation between wholesale and retail prices is not a simple one.

Of imported materials, many have fallen in price, including cotton which influences the aggregate greatly. The falls in rubber and petroleum are noticeable.

Sauerbeck's index-number, given at the bottom of the table, is obtained by averaging the changes in wholesale market prices of 45 selected commodities, as sold in England. In times of rapid movement, especially when food as a whole has a different course to materials as a whole, price index-numbers are liable to be uncertain and unduly dependent on accidents of arrangement. It is interesting to see that Sauerbeck's numbers up to October 1914 move very closely with import prices. In December the import prices are more influenced by the fall in the price of raw materials. Close correspondence with export prices is not to be expected, since exports are dominated by manufactured goods, which hardly enter into Sauerbeck's numbers.

There is nothing in this table that will enable us to forecast the prices of the coming months; but the lessons drawn already (p. 30) as to the apparent adequacy of the supplies of most goods should tend to remove alarm.

CHAPTER IV

TRADE WITH SPECIAL COUNTRIES

THE totals of imports from and exports to individual countries are not published monthly, and we are dependent on those cases where commodities are shown separately for countries, if we wish to study movements month by month; but *quarterly* statements are issued in the monthly accounts for January (published Feb. 8th), April, July and October, which show the divisions of imports, exports and re-exports among countries. Such tables are thus a month later than those which relate to commodities. For the complete division by commodities of each country's trade with the United Kingdom, we have to wait for the Annual Statement of Trade published in the summer, and in that the years are not sub-divided into months or quarters. Consequently we shall never know the immediate effect of the war on the trade with any special country, for the third quarter of 1914 contains more than five weeks' pre-war trade; the nearest that we can do is to watch the monthly shipping records (which distinguish countries) and the movements of particular commodities.

In the table, p. 49, the values of imports and exports are shown, for each country where either annual total reaches £10,000,000, for the whole years 1913 and 1914 and for the third and fourth quarters of 1914. For comparison with the quarterly figures, an estimate of "normal" trade has been made showing the values that would have been recorded in each case, if the trade of the third and fourth quarters of 1914 had formed the same proportion of the trade of the first half of 1914, as that of the latter quarters of 1913 bore to that of the first half of 1913; in brief, on the assumptions that the seasonal movements in 1914 and 1913 had been the same, and that trade had continued on a raised or lowered level in those countries that showed an upward or downward movement early in the year.

(1) BELLIGERENT COUNTRIES

Germany and Austria-Hungary together sent 11·4 per cent. of the total imports and received 8·6 per cent. of the total exports of produce of the United Kingdom in 1913; the corresponding percentages for Russia, France and Belgium together were 14·3 and 11·4. With Germany and Austria the trade of the second half of 1914 is just what we should expect, *i.e.*, about $\frac{5}{13}$ths of the normal in the third quarter and none in the fourth quarter, except that there was very little exportation to Austria in July. With Russia we only managed the equivalent of about seven weeks' trade in the third quarter, and of six weeks' imports and four weeks' exports in the fourth. From France the imports were equivalent to eight weeks' trade in each quarter, while the exports to her were up to ten weeks' trade in the third, and were 10 per cent. over normal in the fourth quarter. As to Belgium, imports and exports were equivalent respectively to nine and seven weeks' normal trade in the third quarter, and they practically ceased before the fall of Antwerp (Oct. 9th).

These countries together account for five-sixths of the diminution of imports in August and September and for more than the whole fall in the fourth quarter; but only one-third of the fall of the value of exports is attributable to them in either quarter.

Of the imports from *Germany* in 1913 (£80,000,000 in all), 20 per cent. or £16,500,000, was food, of which sugar was the most important (11)[1], followed by oats (1); raw materials were valued at £7,000,000, oils and wood being the only commodities in considerable quantities; the bulk (£56,000,000) consisted of manufactured goods in great variety, among which we may distinguish chemical products and coal-dyes (3·5), iron and steel manufactures, machinery, hardware and cutlery (12), woollen yarn and manufactures (2·5), cotton

---

[1] Numbers thus shown are to be read as so many £000,000.

TRADE WITH PRINCIPAL COUNTRIES IN 1913 AND 1914. (*Bullion excluded.*)

Value £00,000s.

| | Imports | | | | Exports of Home Produce | | | | Actual Year's Trade | | | |
| | 3rd Quarter | | 4th Quarter | | 3rd Quarter | | 4th Quarter | | Imports | | Exports | |
	Normal	Actual 1914	Normal	Actual 1914	Normal	Actual 1914	Normal	Actual 1914	1913	1914	1913	1914
Germany	197	76	218	0	103	45	107	0	804	469	407	231
Austria-Hungary	14	6	19		11	0	11	0	77	44	45	27
Russia	138	77	118	52	68	33	60	20	403	281	181	139
France	113	69	112	70	65	39	68	76	464	378	289	259
Belgium	56	35	61	12	30	15	30	2	234	161	132	83
Total : Belligerent	518	263	528	134	277	132	276	98	1982	1333	1054	739
Sweden	42	32	41	51	22	18	21	22	142	142	82	77
Netherlands	61	62	64	66	34	24	41	28	236	243	164	134
Spain	28	28	39	44	13	15	14	12	144	141	79	64
Italy	20	15	23	27	34	26	34	28	81	87	146	129
China [1]	13	16	11	12	48	28	42	18	47	48	148	130
Japan	11	11	11	9	50	18	22	15	44	41	145	84
U.S.A.	246	240	483	442	86	88	110 [3]	76	1417	1386	293	342
Brazil	12	10	18	18	18	12	17	10	100	80	125	63
Argentina	89	79	63	112	48	27	48	23	425	372	226	146
Egypt	21	16	84	36	25	16	27	12	214	171	98	78
Other Foreign Countries	241	233	257	325	180	126	177	103	940	1050	749	600
Total : Non-Belligerent	784	742	1094	1142	558	398	553	347	3790	3761	2245	1847
British India [2]	118	121	135	124	183	156	183	124	484	434	703	630
Canada	98	109	77	106	49	44	46	33	305	314	238	173
South Africa	22	18	34	19	55	43	55	41	123	108	222	187
Australia	78	75	116	80	89	85	87	74	381	370	345	336
New Zealand	50	42	15	27	23	26	23	21	203	230	108	94
Rest of Empire	101	97	93	117	92	69	110	57	419	425	337	296
Total : Empire	467	462	470	473	491	423	504	350	1915	1881	1953	1716
Grand Total	1789	1467	2092	1749	1326	953	1833	794	7687	6974	5252	4802

[1] Excluding Hong-Kong. [2] Not including Ceylon. [3] See p. 51.

Note. The statistics for Turkey, belligerent during a great part of the fourth quarter are, in the order of the columns of the table 12, 8, 24, 10; 29, 11, 30, 1; 54, 40; 78, 59. These include European and Asiatic Turkey.

B.

4

(7·5), silk (2·5), leather and its products (3), glass (1), toys (1), zinc (1·7), copper (·6), paper (1·7). Our exports to Germany were only valued at £41,000,000, together with re-exports (wool, rubber, lard, coffee, jute, etc.) to the value of £20,000,000. Of food and materials, fish (3), coal (5·3) and wool (1·4) are the only important commodities. The manufactures exported were as miscellaneous as the corresponding imports but only half the value (£27,000,000); among these were metals and their products (3), wool:—tops (1), yarn (5), and manufactures (2),— cotton-yarn, etc. (5·7), and manufactures (2·4). It is noticeable that we bought very much more cotton manufactures than we sold.

With *Austria* trade was on a very much smaller scale; more than half the value of imports was due to sugar; of the exports, coal (·9), cotton and woollen manufactures (1), metal products, machinery and ships (1), account for the greater part.

With *France* the principal items of trade in 1913 were exports of coal (£9,000,000), textile products (4), and iron products, including steel and machinery (4). Among imports, food and drink were worth £9,000,000, wine, butter, fruit and vegetables accounting for a great part of this, raw materials (wool, wood, etc.) amounted to £7,000,000, and manufactures to nearly £30,000,000, including silk (6), woollens (5), apparel (3), motor-cars (2).

From *Belgium* we received in 1913 food and raw materials to the value of £6,000,000, among which the only important item was flax (£1,330,000), and manufactures worth £17,000,000, including iron products (4), textiles (3). Exports to Belgium are a miscellany, principally of manufactures.

The trade from *Russia* is more important. Among food imports, worth over £15,000,000 in 1913, we find eggs (5), cereals (5), and butter (4). Raw materials amounted to nearly £23,000,000, and included wood (nearly 14) and flax (3·3); oils, seeds, hides, wool, hemp and manganese are also important; manufactures are negligible. Our exports are relatively small and consist mainly of herrings (2), coal (4·4), iron, steel and machinery (5), and textiles (2).

These five belligerent countries took in 1913 about one-sixth of our exported manufactures.

Trade with *Turkey* fell off greatly in the third quarter. The principal imports are barley and wool, while cotton goods account for a great part of the exports.

(2) OTHER FOREIGN COUNTRIES

The falling off in export trade in the third quarter of the year was by no means confined to that with belligerent countries. Of our more important foreign customers the United States and Spain were the only ones who approached the normal level, already a high one in the case of the former, but low for the latter. Sweden, the Netherlands and Italy, China, Japan and Egypt had bought nearly the same values in the first halves of 1914 and of 1913, but shipments to these (especially China and Japan) fell off greatly in August. Export trade to Brazil and to Argentina was unusually low before July, but attained a still greater deficit. The other countries, undistinguished in the table, had received as much as usual in the first six months of 1914, but took only two-thirds of the normal quantity in the third quarter of 1914. In all, to the non-belligerent countries was sent an equivalent of nine weeks' trade in the third quarter of 1914; under the circumstances the loss of only four weeks' trade was a considerable achievement.

Imports from this group showed a deficit of only one-nineteenth in the third quarter; the loss amounted to £1,000,000 only in the case of Sweden; Italy and Egypt followed with about £500,000 each.

In the fourth quarter exports were only equivalent to about eight weeks' normal trade, even when we withdraw the assumption that U.S.A. would normally have increased her purchases in the autumn of 1914 as much as in the previous autumn, which was necessary for uniformity in the table[1]. The smallness of the shipments to Argentina and to Egypt is specially noticeable.

[1] Exports to U.S.A. (£00,000s), 1913, 1st 6 months, 139; 3rd quarter, 67; 4th quarter, 87. 1914, 1st 6 months, 178; 3rd quarter, 88; 4th quarter, 76.

Imports on the other hand increased to above the normal in most cases, but this movement is more than accounted for by the rise of prices; the quantity actually diminished.

(3) THE EMPIRE

The value of the aggregate imports from the Empire in the third quarter of 1914 was only 1 per cent. below normal; an excess from Canada of £1,100,000 balanced defects from New Zealand and Australia, though of course the commodities were not of the same kind; a trifling increase from India balanced a fall from South Africa.

The position as to exports was not quite so favourable, but in all the fall in August and September only amounted to two weeks' trade. The check in the cotton trade with India accounts for two-thirds of the fall with that country. Exports to Canada, Australia and New Zealand were nearly normal, those to South Africa showed a decrease. The drop in exports to the Crown Colonies was nearly universal; Hong-Kong, where the great part of the consignments is for re-export, accounts for very little of it.

Both with imports and exports the fourth quarter repeated the phenomena of the third. Imports came as usual, except that India and Australia fell away from their amounts of the previous autumn, and Canada, New Zealand and other countries (Ceylon, the Straits, West Indies, Guiana) filled up the deficit. But the very slight increase in the total was not enough to pay the war insurance, and quantities had decreased. In exports there was a falling off all round, the equivalent of four weeks' trade being lost. In the half year exports to non-belligerent foreign countries lost the equivalent of three weeks' more trade than exports to the Empire. As to imports, values were nearly normal in both groups.

CONCLUSION

While the smallness of the diminution in the value of imports from non-belligerent countries is very remarkable, it must be remembered that this value (estimated at the ports of arrival) includes freights, and is also, especially in the fourth quarter, inflated by higher prices in the countries of origin. But if we make allowance for these changes and estimate roughly the quantities as on p. 42, we may still say that during the five months beginning August 1914 less than two weeks' imports was lost from the Empire and from non-belligerent foreign countries, and that even of this much was simply delayed by congestion at the docks. The enemy's efforts to check our supplies from countries not actually at war have thus had less effect than a minor trade crisis and about as much as a moderately serious strike of transport workers.

With exports, with which the enemy has not directly concerned himself, the position is different, and trade has gone back to a definitely lower scale, though the aggregate to all countries is still well above that of, say, 1902, the date of the beginning of the fiscal controversy. Part of this fall is due to the special conditions of the cotton-trade (p. 35) and is likely to be recovered to some extent; part was due to the disorganization of the foreign exchanges in the early months of the war, part to the closing of the important markets of Germany and Austria, to the hindrance of trade with Russia, the destruction of Belgium, and the pre-occupation of France in affairs of war. Judging from the trade of December 1914 and January 1915 the scale of our exports of home-produce has shrunk so as to cause a diminution (if there is no change) of about £230,000,000 per annum, of which £100,000,000 is due to loss of trade with Germany, Austria, Turkey, Belgium and Russia; re-exports have also diminished ; meanwhile imports approximate to their old level of value. This shrinkage is ultimately connected with the withdrawal of vast numbers of men from production entirely and the diversion of another great number to providing the munitions and other necessaries of war. The smaller number who are producing part of the manufactured goods which we generally import may be balanced against the reduction in the number generally engaged in producing luxuries.

Reverting to the discussion on p. 16, we see that the

excess of the value of imports over that of exports will tend
to reach £350,000,000 or £400,000,000 a year. So far as can
be judged this total is little if at all more than the amounts
due as interests, profits, etc., from abroad, together with the
high earnings of shipping, which at once cause part of the
excess and help to meet it. It is not necessary to assume
as yet that we are becoming a debtor instead of a creditor
nation and that we are realising investments abroad to pay
for our imports, but there cannot be any great margin at the
present levels of trade. So far the great part of the reduction
of exports may be attributed to the cessation of new external
investment, and the remainder to the actual diminution of
the total value of imports reckoned at the country of their
origin. The apparent near equality of the values of imports
in January 1914 and January 1915 is due to the inflation of
freights, mainly payable to British owners. The first sign of
difficulty will, of course, be shown by a movement against
us of the foreign exchanges and a pressure to export gold,
phenomena present with Germany since the beginning of the
war.

Finally, it appears that our dependence on foreign and
colonial supplies and our possible vulnerability at sea have
had as yet hardly any visible effect on our production or
consumption; for prices must rise, credit be temporarily
disorganized, capital cease to accumulate, production be
checked and industry diverted, in any country engaged in a
serious war, whether it be insular or continental, trading or
self-sufficient.

ADDENDUM

TRADE IN JANUARY 1915, COMPARED WITH JANUARY 1914

Value £00,000s.

	Imports		Exports (Home Produce)		Re-exports	
	1914	1915	1914	1915	1914	1915
Food, drink and tobacco	237	311	24	20	14	23
Raw Materials	281	232	60	34	56	29
Manufactures	157	128	385	217	26	16
Total (including miscellaneous)..	680	674	478	282	96	69

SELECTED IMPORTS. QUANTITIES

	Unit	1914 Jan.	1915 Jan.
Wheat	100,000 cwts.	72	78
Beef	10,000 cwts.	72	53
Mutton	,, ,,	41	36
Cotton	1,000,000 lbs.	307	300
Wool	100,000 lbs.	1006	1040
Flax	100 tons	98	41

SELECTED EXPORTS. QUANTITIES

	Unit	1914 Jan.	1915 Jan.
Coal	100,000 tons	58	36
Iron and Steel Manufactures ..	1,000 tons	455	225
Machinery	1,000 tons	65	30
Cotton: Yarn	100,000 lbs.	191	138
Piece	10,000,000 yds.	69	35
Woollen Piece	100,000 yds.	118	60
Worsted Piece	100,000 yds.	100	67

Printed in the United States
By Bookmasters